A Lighthouse Story

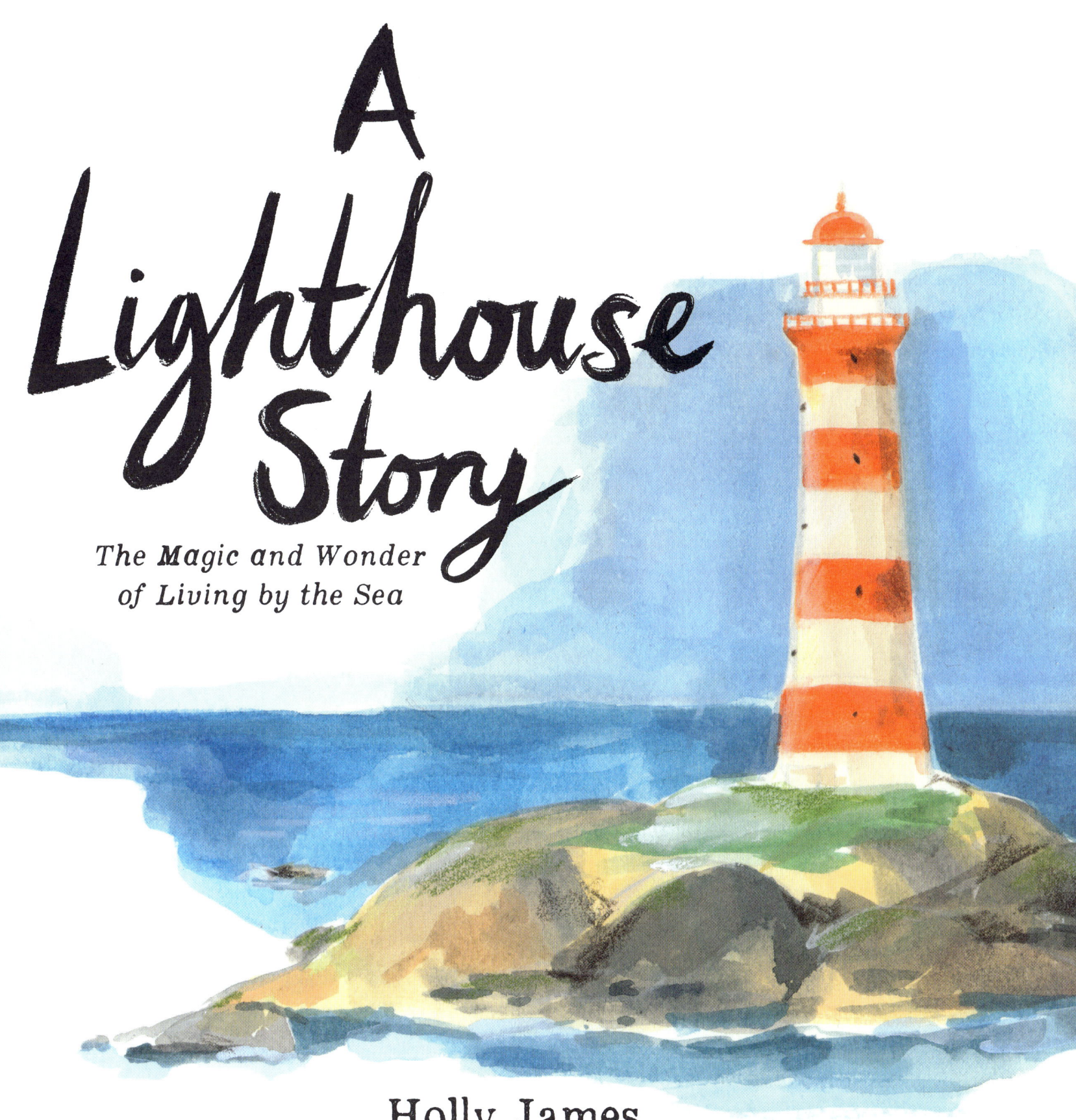

A Lighthouse Story

The Magic and Wonder of Living by the Sea

Holly James
Illustrated by
Laura Chamberlain

BLOOMSBURY
CHILDREN'S BOOKS

LONDON OXFORD NEW YORK NEW DELHI SYDNEY

On bright summer days, Eva visits her Grandad.

Getting there is no ordinary journey.
Eva must travel across the sea.
Waves crash and splash, rocking
the small boat. Eva holds on tight.
She can see Grandad in the distance.

On the rocky island in the middle of the sea, surrounded by crashing waves, Eva's Grandad lives in the lighthouse.

Sailors use lighthouse patterns to tell where they are on the coastline. Some lighthouses have red stripes, others have thick black ones and some are just a plain, bright white to make them stand out against the dark cliffs.

Eva thought that Grandad's lighthouse was the most beautiful of all. She loved visiting him and spent every minute asking millions of questions all about lighthouses.

It was a lot of work to look after a lighthouse, and Grandad had a long list of chores to keep Eva busy.

First, they had to clean the powerful lens that made the light shine far and wide. If it got dirty or cloudy, sailors might not be able to find their way in the dark.

Eva loved Grandad's old light clcaning box.

All day, they watched the weather: the shapes of the clouds, the rain, the brewing storms. Grandad wrote everything down in his dog-eared and scruffy logbook.

CLOUD FORMATIONS

HIGH CLOUDS

Cirrus

Cirrocumulus

MIDDLE CLOUDS

Altostratus

Altocumulus

LOW CLOUDS

Stratocumulus

Cumulonimbus

Stratus

Cumulus

Nimbostratus

On foggy days, Grandad turned on the foghorn.
It made a low sound to warn sailors of the rocky
coastline in case they couldn't see the lighthouse's
shining beam through the mist.

All around the lighthouse,
Eva spotted birds and ocean life.

Migrating birds soared overhead, back
and forth at the same times each year.

Seals lounged on rocks and played games in the shallows.

Rock pools were home to extraordinary life: scuttling crabs, slimy seaweed and spiky starfish.

And large schools of fish swam through the water, their scales sparkling in the sunshine.

When the sun set, the lighthouse lamp burned brightly to show the hidden paths across the ocean. Grandad's lighthouse beamed out three short flashes of light.

Others have different patterns. It's how sailors can tell which lighthouse is which.

Before bedtime, Grandad checked his watch to make sure that the flashes coming from the lamp were timed just right.

On the clearest night, Eva and Grandad stood at the top
of the tower and counted all the stars in the sky.

Grandad picked out constellations and told Eva how
ancient seafarers navigated through the seas, chasing dogs
and bears through the night sky.

One night, a storm came.

The bright beam of light from the lamp guided sailors to safety …

... and Grandad's lighthouse
protected him and Eva against
the gusts and gales.

Down, down, down they went, past the watch room and Grandad's bedroom, to where it was safe and warm.

While they waited for the storm to pass, Grandad read
Eva stories from the sea: tales of daring rescues and
brave lighthouse keepers.

Eva's favourite was the true story of Grace Darling – a girl who was brought to live in a lighthouse when she was just a baby.

One night, when Grace was grown up, there was a terrible storm.

From her window, she spotted a shipwreck on the rocks below.

Running to the telescope, she searched among the jagged rocks and splintered wood, and as the light of morning began to shine, Grace spotted survivors.

Grace and her father ran to their rowing boat and pushed it out to sea.

They battled the storm, conquered waves and bravely fought through winds.

While Grace kept the boat as still as possible, her father pulled the survivors on board …

… and brought them back to the safety of their lighthouse. Grace was a hero.

When Eva went back home, she worried that Grandad would be lonely all by himself.

But she had seen how he could send messages to other lighthouses by flashing the light in the tower. Sometimes voices from nearby ships crackled on the radio in his watch room. And Eva always remembered to write him letters.

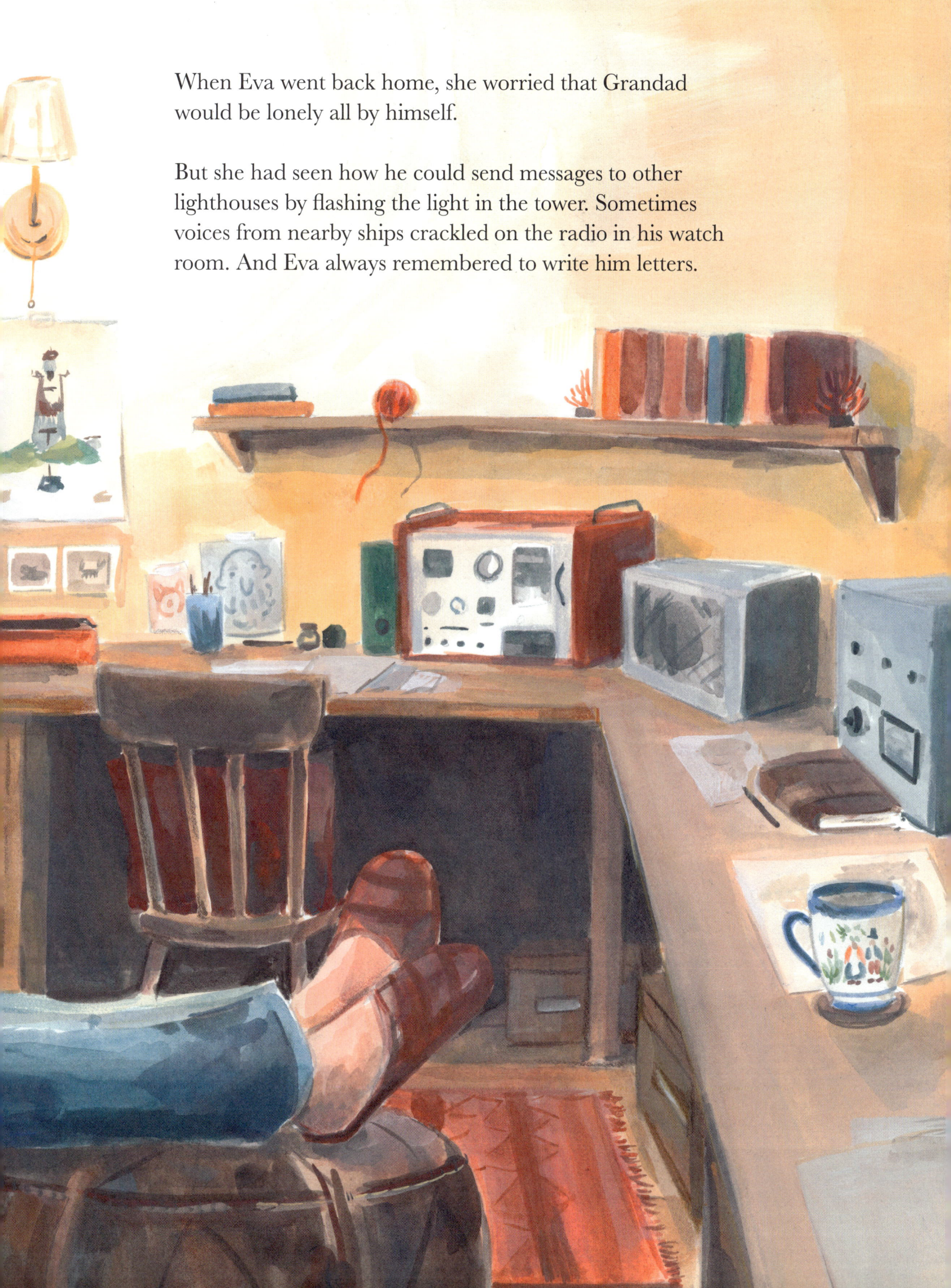

Eva proudly told everyone she met all about her trips to see Grandad and his wonderful lighthouse.

'Grandad's lighthouse has to be as tall as possible, so the light can shine for miles and miles.'

The highter up a light is, the further away you can see it.

If a lighthouse is too short, the curve of the earth gets in the way.

If you stood 15 ft above the horizon and the lighthouse is 100ft tall, in clear weather you could see the light 16 nautical miles (nearly 30 km) away.

'The tower is shaped like a giant, upright rolling pin to take on MIGHTY storms and GIGANTIC waves.'

Look at these photos that a local fisherman took!

A copper wire connects the spire to the ground. When the lightning hits the spire, the electricity travels down the wire to the ground.

Love Grandad x

'A spire stretches from the top of Grandad's lighthouse to catch dangerous lightning and keep the tower safe during storms.'

Eva told stories of sitting with Grandad and seeing the incredible view from the top of the tower.

Eva couldn't wait to visit Grandad and
his lighthouse again.

The Lighthouse Keeper's Handbook

Why were lighthouses first created?

From ancient times, lighthouses' bright fires have lit up the coast, shining out even on the darkest nights and the stormiest days to guide sailors as they brave the seas.

What are they for?

Every lighthouse provides a friendly beacon, leading ships into a safe harbour or warning them to stay away from dangerous rocks or hidden hazards. They protect lives and allow people to sail the seas safely.

What has been used to light the lamp?

At first, lighthouses had wood fires burning out in the open. Then people used candles or oil lamps in glass lanterns. Today's lighthouses are lit by modern, efficient electric light bulbs.

Candle chandelier

Bonfire

Oil lamp

Electric light

How does the beam of light travel so far?

It's all down to a clever arrangement of glass called a Fresnel lens, which is a pattern of curved glass rings around the light source. When the light shines, the glass bends the light rays, into one very powerful, straight, far-reaching beam.

Modern Lighthouses

How did electricity change lighthouses?

Keepers no longer had to carry heavy fuel to keep the light burning, but now lighthouses would need a reliable source of electricity. Many had their own generators well before electricity was widely available.

Why don't lighthouses need keepers anymore?

Running a lighthouse was once a gruelling, round-the-clock task. Now the lights are electric and are set to turn and flash automatically. They can even be remote-controlled from miles away.

What are lighthouses used for now?

Many lighthouses are still working to rescue shipwrecked travellers. They are also visited by tourists who can sometimes see inside the towers.

Famous Lighthouses of the World

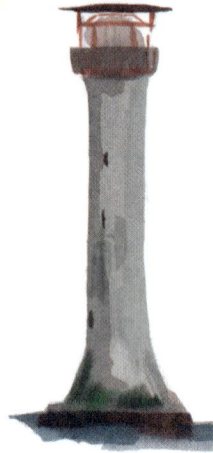

Eddystone
England

This was the first lighthouse to be built on a small rock in the open sea. It is shaped like a tree trunk, so it is strong in fierce winds.

Longstone
England

This was the home of Grace Darling. You can visit it and see the tiny bedroom from which she spotted a ship sinking in a terrible storm.

Bell Rock
Scotland

This is the world's oldest surviving original lighthouse. It has stood for over 200 years without needing repair.

Fastnet
Ireland

This is known as the 'teardrop of Ireland' because it was the last glimpse of home seen by emigrants sailing from Ireland to America.

Tower of Hercules
Spain

This is the oldest working lighthouse in the world. It was built by the ancient Romans in the second century.

The Cordouan Lighthouse
France

This lighthouse was fitted out with a royal bedroom for King Louis XIV in case he wanted to stay. It was the first lighthouse to have a Fresnel lens, in 1823.

Slettnes Lighthouse
Norway

This is the world's most northerly mainland lighthouse. For a few months in summer, the sun never sets and there is no need for the light to be switched on.

Victory Lighthouse
Italy

This claims to have the most powerful beam of any lighthouse. It is also a memorial to sailors who died in the First World War.

The Statue of Liberty
USA

The Statue of Liberty's torch is a symbolic beacon of light and freedom, and for a few years was a real, working lighthouse. It was the first electric lighthouse in the US.

Boston Light
USA

Today this is the only lighthouse in the US with a keeper. It was America's first lighthouse, and helped Boston grow into a big, successful city.

Les Éclaireurs Lighthouse
Argentina

This is so far south that it is known as the 'lighthouse at the end of the world'. It sits on a small craggy rock surrounded by seabirds.

Macquarie Lighthouse
Australia

This is Australia's oldest lighthouse and has been shining outside Sydney Harbour ever since 1818. It was one of the first lighthouses to go electric.

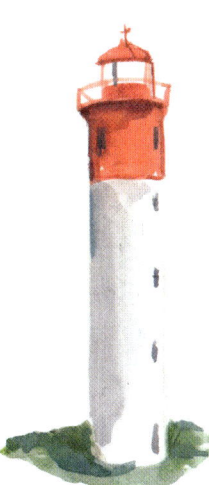

The Pharos of Alexandria
Egypt

This magnificent ancient Egyptian lighthouse was one of the seven wonders of the world. It was over 100 m high.

Jeddah Light
Saudi Arabia

This lighthouse is the tallest in the world today, at 133 m. The globe-shaped room near the top is a control room for Jeddah port.

Enoshima Sea Candle
Japan

This futuristic-looking lighthouse has an unusual cone shape and is built of metal and glass. On winter nights it is lit up with colourful light displays.

The Umhlanga Lighthouse
South Africa

Speedy workers built this lighthouse in just 4 days and 19 hours! It has never had a keeper but staff at a hotel next door take care of the tower.

Inside a Lighthouse

Lens

The lens makes light shine far and bright. It is a large, cylinder-shaped Fresnel lens. It magnifies the bulb's rays.

Lamp

Behind the lens is quite a small electric bulb. Some lighthouses have solar energy charging giant batteries that power the electricity for the bulb.

Tower

The tower is tall so it can be seen from far away. The rooms and workings of the lighthouse are inside.

Watch room

This control room is underneath the lantern room. It has big windows so the keeper can watch out without going outside.

Foghorn
When it's very foggy it's time for a loud trumpet-shaped instrument called a foghorn to honk, or blare out.

Morse code
Morse code is a way of sending messages using light flashes or bursts of sound, in a combination of short and long pulses (dots and dashes).

Maritime signal flag
Ships can use coloured flags to send messages clearly and quickly. There is a code to say what the different colours and patterns mean.

Logbook
The logbook is for keeping daily records of every detail seen or measured from the lighthouse: the weather, ships passing, wildlife spotted and the keeper's jobs.

BLOOMSBURY CHILDREN'S BOOKS
Bloomsbury Publishing Plc
50 Bedford Square, London, WC1B 3DP, UK
29 Earlsfort Terrace, Dublin 2

BLOOMSBURY, BLOOMSBURY CHILDREN'S BOOKS and the Diana
logo are trademarks of Bloomsbury Publishing Plc
First published in Great Britain 2022 by Bloomsbury Publishing Plc
Text copyright © Bloomsbury, 2022
Illustrations copyright © Laura Chamberlain, 2022

A catalogue record for this book is available from the British Library

ISBN: 978-1-5266-2412-3;

2 4 6 8 10 9 7 5 3 1

Printed and bound in China by Leo Paper Products, Heshan, Guangdong

To find out more about our authors and books visit www.bloomsbury.com
and sign up for our newsletters